THE PARALLEL BETWEEN THE ENGLISH AND AMERICAN CIVIL WARS

T0345986

THE PARALLEL BETWEEN THE ENGLISH AND AMERICAN CIVIL WARS

THE REDE LECTURE

DELIVERED IN THE SENATE HOUSE, CAMBRIDGE
ON 14 JUNE 1910

BY

CHARLES HARDING FIRTH, M.A

REGIUS PROFESSOR OF MODERN HISTORY, OXFORD

Cambridge :
at the University Press
1910

CAMBRIDGE
UNIVERSITY PRESS

University Printing House, Cambridge CB2 8BS, United Kingdom

Cambridge University Press is part of the University of Cambridge.

It furthers the University's mission by disseminating knowledge in the pursuit of education, learning and research at the highest international levels of excellence.

www.cambridge.org
Information on this title: www.cambridge.org/9781107673618

© Cambridge University Press 1910

First published 1910
First paperback edition 2014

A catalogue record for this publication is available from the British Library

ISBN 978-1-107-67361-8 Paperback

THE PARALLEL BETWEEN THE
ENGLISH AND AMERICAN
CIVIL WARS

HISTORICAL parallels are pitfalls for the politician, because history never really repeats itself. One event may resemble another event, one situation another, although there is an interval of scores of years, or perhaps centuries, between them. Yet the conditions under which those events happened can never be the same, since change of place and progress of time forbid it. If we search a little we shall find that the superficial resemblances conceal fundamental differences, just as, when we look beneath the surface of things, we shall often perceive a real likeness where at first sight only the dissimilarity struck the eye.

Suppose then that we take events which possess some general resemblance, and examine into the reasons why they resemble each other, and the extent to which they differ, and consider why they differ. Such a comparison is often profitable for the historian. It helps him to understand the real character of both events better; it brings out the special characteristics of each, the essential qualities which distinguish those particular events from each other, and from others of the same kind.

It is for this reason that I have chosen an historical parallel as my subject to-day. The two events which I shall try to compare or contrast have a special interest for me— one is the first political event in which I was interested as a boy, the other has been the study of my manhood. Their comparison has often been suggested by American writers. Mr J. F. Rhodes, for instance, in his *History of the American Civil War*, says, "The most interesting and instructive parallel to this period of our history is the great Civil War in England."

The parallel was often suggested while the American Civil War was in progress: it occurred to some of the actors themselves. Once President Lincoln was pressed to offer terms to the South, and said that he could not treat with parties in arms against the government. The Confederate emissary argued that it had been often done, "especially by Charles I when at war with the British Parliament." Lincoln nimbly avoided the pitfall. "I do not profess," said he, "to be posted in history. On all such matters I will turn you over to Seward. All I distinctly recollect about Charles I is that he lost his head in the end[1]."

It is natural that there should be many points of similarity. Take two races of the same stock, both trained by free institutions and both nurtured by the same creeds, heat them in the fire of political passions, subject them to the strain and pressure of civil war, and we should expect results of much the same kind to follow.

But the conditions under which the two

[1] James Ford Rhodes, *History of the United States, from the Compromise of* 1850, iii. 356, v. 70.

experiments were conducted were not the same. One struggle had for its theatre a small island, the other half a continent; between the one struggle and the other two centuries elapsed, during which time institutions founded on the same basis developed in different directions, and two different forms of society grew up from the same root. So the later struggle took a different shape from the earlier one, and raised new problems.

In the political causes of the two struggles there is a certain resemblance. In each case the formal cause of the quarrel was the question of sovereignty. In America the question was, What share of sovereignty rightly belonged to individual States and what to the Federal government? In England the question was, What share of sovereignty rightly belonged to the King, and what to the Parliament? Some would put the problem differently, and say that it was a question which of two partners was the real sovereign. In America the issue was less simple than it was in England; it became a controversy as to the nature of the Federal government. "The sovereignty is in the several States," said Calhoun, on behalf of the South, "and our system is a union of 24 sovereign powers under a constitutional compact, not of a divided sovereignty between the States severally and the United States." The doctrine of the North, as maintained by Webster, was "that the constitution of the United States is not a league, confederation or compact between the people of the several States in their sovereign capacity, but a government proper founded on the adoption of the people."

In England, as Ireton said, the controversy was not what the nature of the "supreme trust" was, but whether the "supreme trust" was in King or Parliament. "The ground of the war was not a difference in what the supreme magistracy was, but whether it was in the King alone[1]."

Let us look beyond the formal ground of

---

[1] *Clarke Papers*, ii. 80.

the quarrel to its real causes. In both countries, directly or indirectly, the struggle was a struggle for the maintenance of a free government, but in England the problem took the simplest and most elementary form. The question was, whether the will of one man should determine the destinies of a whole people. So at least the leaders of the republicans asserted, seeing more clearly than other men what the real issue would become. "I do not think," said Harry Marten to Mr Hyde, "one man wise enough to govern us all," a word, says Hyde, "which would at the time have been abhorred by the whole nation." "The question in dispute between the King's party and us," said Ludlow, "was as I apprehended, whether the King should govern as a God by his will, and the nation be governed by force like beasts, or whether the people should be governed by laws made by themselves, and live under a government derived from their own consent[1]."

---

[1] Clarendon, *Life*, i. 92 ; Ludlow, *Memoirs*, ed. 1894, i. 206.

In America it was not a question between one man and a people, but whether the majority or the minority of the people should govern. "A constitutional majority is the only true sovereign of a free people," said Lincoln in his Inaugural. It was necessary, he declared, to prove this once for all. "We must settle this question now—whether in a free government the minority have a right to break it up whenever they choose. If we fail it will go far to prove the incapacity of the people to govern themselves." It was necessary "to demonstrate to the world that those who can fairly carry an election can also suppress a rebellion; that ballots are the rightful and peaceful successors of bullets; and that when ballots have fairly and constitutionally decided there can be no successful appeal back to bullets."

Regarded thus the war was not a war for dominion, but one in defence of "a people's government," a war undertaken in order that "the government of the people, for the people, by the people" should not perish, and therefore essentially "a people's contest."

In America the claim of the minority to break up the government, if they could not direct it, linked the maintenance of free government and the maintenance of the union together. "I have thought it proper," said Lincoln, "to keep the integrity of our union prominent as the primary object of the contest on our side." The "war was commenced by the South to destroy our union," and "the administration accepted the war thus commenced for the sole avowed object of preserving our union." Any nation which accepted the principles of the Southern leaders must cease to be a nation. "If a minority will secede rather than acquiesce they make a precedent which in turn will divide and ruin them; for a minority of their own will secede from them whenever a majority refuses to be controlled by such a minority[1]."

---

[1] See Nicolay and Hay's *Life of Lincoln*, iii. 336; iv. 258, 373, 374; v. 204; vii. 384; viii. 202; ix. 356, 380.

In England the maintenance of the integrity of the State was not one of the questions at issue. Our Civil War produced the union of England, Scotland and Ireland, but excepting in the war for the reconquest of Ireland there is no trace of that feeling against the dismemberment of the State which wrought so powerfully in America. "Remember, ye hypocrites," said Cromwell in his declaration to the Irish clergy, "Ireland was once united to England. You broke that union." While Ireland was a dependency which had shaken off the bond which linked it to England, Scotland was an independent nation linked to England merely by the accident of hereditary succession. The two countries were conquered and united to England because the King called in the aid of the Scots and Irish to break down the resistance of England to arbitrary rule. "The quarrel," said Cromwell in 1649, "is brought to this state, that we can hardly return unto that tyranny that we were formerly under the yoke of, but we must at the same time be

9

subject to the kingdom of Scotland, or the kingdom of Ireland, for the bringing in of the King[1]." Thus the conflict for self-government developed into a struggle for national independence, and ended in the attainment of national unity. Yet the attainment was temporary only; the union of the three kingdoms lasted but seven years, and it was not permanently achieved till 140 years later.

Here we see the two conflicts producing similar results, though in one case the result was incidental, and in the other it was the thing fought for from the beginning. Both in the English and American conflict there were causes of discord which lay deeper than the avowed reasons for fighting, and made the quarrel irreconcilable. In England the purely political question about which the war began might have been settled without a war if it had not been for the religious difficulty—for the demand of the Puritans for ecclesiastical changes. Their

---

[1] Carlyle's *Cromwell*, ed. Lomas, i. 404; ii. 8.

attack on the national church gave the King a party, and made war possible. As the conflict proceeded the religious question grew in importance, and freedom of conscience became by degrees the only solution of the problem. "Religion," said Cromwell in 1655, "was not the thing at first contested for, but God brought it to that issue at last; and gave it unto us by way of redundancy; and at last it proved that which was the most dear to us." "Undoubtedly," he said a year later, "this is the peculiar interest all this while contested for[1]." It became so dear to the Puritans that some were willing to sacrifice political liberty for the sake of it.

In the American struggle the question at issue was not the rights of conscience but the common rights of humanity. Slavery was directly and obviously the cause of the conflict, as men had seen for years that it would be. "Our political problem now," wrote Lincoln in 1855, "is, can we as a nation

[1] Carlyle's *Cromwell*, ed. Lomas, ii. 154, 417, 536.

continue together permanently—for ever—half slave and half free? The problem is too mighty for me." Three years later he had found the answer. "A house divided against itself cannot stand. I believe this government cannot endure permanently, half slave and half free. I do not expect the union to be dissolved—I do not expect the house to fall—but I do expect it will cease to be divided. It will become all one thing or all the other[1]."

Many of those to whom human freedom was of paramount importance were willing to sacrifice the integrity of the nation for it. To them the abolition of slavery was a new religion "based upon the Bible and carried out with a millennial fervour." Garrison took as his motto "No union with slaveholders," declared the constitution "a covenant with death and an agreement with hell" and publicly burnt a copy of it at a meeting of Abolitionists. Advocated thus, the anti-slavery movement set the feeling of the

[1] Nicolay and Hay, i. 391; ii. 137, 150.

12

nation against it, and was too weak to accomplish its purpose.

Lincoln's great achievement was to combine the cause of human freedom with the cause of the union. At the beginning of the war he kept the two causes separate, and put the integrity of the nation first. "My paramount object in this struggle," he wrote in August 1862, "is to save the union, and is not either to save or to destroy slavery. If I could save the union without freeing any slave, I would do it; and if I could save it by freeing all the slaves, I would do it; and if I could save it by freeing some and leaving others alone, I would do it." When the right moment came he bound the two causes together, employing the anti-slavery feeling to maintain the union, and the union feeling to secure human freedom. The proclamation of September 22, 1862, announced the intention of emancipating the slaves in the rebellious States, and on January 1, 1863, the Emancipation Edict followed[1]. Military

---

[1] Nicolay and Hay, vi. 153, 168, 414, 430.

necessity was the ground on which Lincoln justified emancipation, just as in England military necessity was the first and the most effective plea for toleration. "Honest men," wrote Cromwell to Parliament after Naseby, "served you faithfully in this action…. I beseech you not to discourage them. He that ventures his life for the liberty of his country I wish he trust God for the liberty of his conscience, and you for the liberty he fights for." But Cromwell when he attained power could never succeed in reconciling the movement for religious liberty and the movement for political liberty. He always declared that the liberty of the people of God and the liberty of the nation were perfectly compatible, and that it was "a pitiful fancy" to think they were inconsistent with each other. The army demanded one and the Parliament the other, and the impossibility of reconciling their demands produced the constitutional struggles of the Protectorate and the anarchy which led up to the Restoration. So while the battles fought in the American Civil

War permanently secured the ends they were fought for, Cromwell's victories were less fruitful.

Let us now turn from the political to the military aspects of the two struggles. There is one obvious difference. The English Civil War was in the main a contest between two parties, the American a contest between two parts of one country. For that reason Mr Goldwin Smith declared that the term "civil war" was hardly appropriate in the case of America, "since this was not a struggle between two parties for the same land, like that between the League and the Huguenots in France, or the Cavaliers and Roundheads in England, but between two communities territorially separate for the land of one of them which the other had taken arms to annex. Only in the border States, in which each of the two parties was struggling for ascendancy, could it be strictly called a civil war[1]."

This is rather hypercritical. A war

[1] Goldwin Smith, *The United States*, p. 249.

between men of the same race, who had lived for three-quarters of a century under the same government, regarded themselves as one nation, and spoke the same language, is essentially a civil war. Defoe's typical Cavalier, who had served in the German wars and returned to fight for the King at Edge-hill and Marston Moor, found that the language was the thing which made him realise what civil war meant. "To hear a man cry for quarter in English moved me to a compassion which I had never been used to."

However, it is true that in America the division was mainly a sectional one. The line drawn across the United States by the Missouri Compromise in 1820, in order to limit the northern extension of slavery—known as Mason and Dixon's line—formed a rough boundary between Federal and Confederate States. Even in England there was some tendency to the geographical division of the contending parties. The text-books say that at the beginning of our war a line drawn from Hull to Portsmouth would have shown which parts of the country supported the King and which the Parliament. But it was not a straight line. "England," writes Dr Gardiner, "was divided by an undulating line which left only the less wealthy and less thickly populated districts of the North and West to Charles."

Between the districts in which one party was practically supreme there lay in each country a debatable land where the two parties struggled for supremacy. In America it was formed by the five border States, Maryland, Virginia, Kentucky, Missouri and Tennessee; in England it was formed by the midland counties and by Yorkshire. In that debatable land most of the great battles took place, and armies swept backwards and forwards till victories in the field settled the possession of the disputed territory. Counties in England played a part analogous to that played by individual States in America. County committees acted on a small scale like the State governments. They enlisted forces of their own and had power to appoint commanders; they levied taxes, raised requisitions, and waged local campaigns against the adherents of the other party. Often these local forces refused to serve outside the boundaries of their shires. Sometimes a county endeavoured to remain neutral. In Cheshire and Yorkshire at the beginning of the war formal treaties of neutrality were signed by the leaders of the two parties. The county of Devon made a truce with the county of Cornwall. Other counties made leagues for mutual defence. On each side there were associations of counties formed on behalf of King or Parliament, of which the most famous was the Eastern Association. The Eastern counties gave the Parliament the same steady and efficient support that their descendants in the New England States gave to the cause of the North.

In very many respects the position of the Parliament resembled that of the Federal government. Both began the war with great advantages. The Parliament, like the North, held the seat of the national government, and controlled whatever central machinery existed. But the possession of London meant much more than the possession of Washington; it was Washington, New York and Boston in one—the headquarters of the administration, the money market, and the intellectual centre united—and it had comparatively a larger population than those three cities put together. Oxford, the seat of the royal government, situated almost on the frontier of the territory which the King held, furnishes a sort of analogy to Richmond; year after year the forces of the Parliament marched against it and failed to take it and its fall marked the end of the war.

These are superficial resemblances. It is more important to remember that the Parliament, like the Federal government, possessed far greater financial resources than its adversary. It held the richest part of the country, most of the capitalists lived in its quarters, the taxes it levied were more productive, and it could raise loans with greater facility. In the American Civil War the possession of mines and foundries and factories was one of the elements in the superiority of the North; in our Civil War the simpler economic organisation of the time made the control of the manufacturing districts less vital.

The Parliament like the Federal government had the disposal of the national navy. It could intercept the supplies which the King sought to draw from the continent, and prevent him from obtaining foreign help. It could capture seaports held by the King, as for instance Portsmouth, or retain seaports besieged by his forces, such as Hull and Plymouth. The English fleet achieved no exploit comparable to the capture of New Orleans by Farragut, could exert no pressure equivalent to that exercised by the Federal blockading squadrons on the Confederacy, but its influence on the course of the war was greater than historians have allowed.

Except at the beginning, the soldiers of

the South were as well armed as those of the North. It was estimated that there were, when the war began, 145,000 muskets in the Southern magazines as against 415,000 in the Northern. What was lacking was soon supplied by the English blockade runners. At first the Parliament, like the Federal government, had the advantage in armament: at Edgehill most of the King's cavalry were armed with swords only, and some hundreds of his foot had clubs instead of pikes or muskets; but the importation of arms from France and Holland soon placed the two armies on an equality.

The great difference between the two Civil Wars was that the United States had a small professional army while England had none at all. In our war a considerable number of the higher officers on both sides had seen service on the continent; Essex, Lindsey, Skippon, Monck, Astley and Hopton are examples. But there was not either in the army of King or Parliament one single regiment of trained men to serve as a nucleus and a model. In America there was a regular army of about 16,000 men, and about 1,200 officers who had received a scientific military training at West Point were available for service. About a fifth of these 1,200 officers sided with their States against the Federal government, while the North had four-fifths of them at its disposal, as well as all the privates. But in organising its armies the North did not make as good use of these regular regiments as it might have done; they remained distinct from the new forces instead of being employed to leaven and discipline them.

In the main therefore the military problem in the English and American Civil Wars was identical; that problem was how to turn a vast mass of untrained men into soldiers with just a handful of trained officers to do it. "I have not really one thorough soldier in my whole army," wrote Sherman in May 1862, "they are all equally green and raw." Some generals forgot that their opponents were in the same position. When General

Macdowell, just before the battle of Bull
Run, asked for a longer time to discipline
his men before attacking the Confederates,
he was answered, "You are green, but they
are green too." In these masses of volunteers,
both in England and America, discipline was
at first absolutely lacking. "Out of my seven
regiments," wrote Sherman in August 1861,
"three are in a state of mutiny, and yesterday
I had my regulars all ready with shotted
guns to fire on our own troops." In the
same way Cromwell complained to the
Suffolk committee that the horse it had
raised "are so mutinous that I may justly
fear they would cut my throat, were it not
that I have honest troops to master them."
Cromwell's great achievement was that he
solved the difficulty of converting raw volunteers into drilled and disciplined soldiers
with more success than any other general of
his time.

At the beginning of the war the Parlia-
mentary cavalry was overmatched by the
Royalist. Cromwell attributed this inferiority

to the bad quality of the men: "the spirits
of such base and mean fellows" were not
"able to encounter gentlemen that have
honour and courage and resolution in them"
and it was necessary to get "men of a spirit
that will go on as far as gentlemen will go,"
men that "had the fear of God before them,
and made some conscience of what they did."
The disparity which at first existed between
the Federal and the Confederate cavalry was
due to a different cause—to physical rather
than moral deficiencies: man for man the
horsemen of the South were better riders
and better shots, and at the time they were
better organised and better led. The
Southern infantry, taking them as a whole,
were better marksmen than those of the
North, owing to the different conditions of
life in the two sections of the country. But
the success of the Southern armies during
the early part of the war was also due to the
difference in the social organisation of South
and North. In the South, as Mr Goldwin
Smith puts it, "the gentry were accustomed

to command, the common people to obey."
The Southern aristocracy furnished regimental officers who were accepted as natural
leaders and loyally followed. In the regiments
of volunteers raised by the North the officers
were usually elected by their men, chosen
for popularity rather than competence, and
as a result indifferently obeyed. The democratic spirit made it difficult for discipline
to take root.

In seventeenth-century England there
was not this difficulty. Like the South, it
was an aristocratic community. Amongst
Roundheads and Cavaliers officers were appointed from above, not elected from below,
and men of birth and property were selected
if they could be obtained. Cromwell was
blamed for appointing a captain of horse who
was not a gentleman. He answered by
admitting that "men of honour and birth"
were best, but complained that they had not
offered themselves. "Seeing it was necessary
the work must go on, better plain men
than none, but best to have men patient of

wants, faithful and conscientious in the employment, and such I hope these will prove themselves to be[1]." They did prove themselves such: they showed that democracy and discipline might be allies, not enemies, and won the war in the process.

In America, Sherman, who also regarded efficiency as the one thing that mattered, dwelt continually on the difficulty of conducting a war under a democratic form of government. He complained that the enforcement of discipline was made impossible, that politicians dictated military movements, that the press betrayed the plans of the generals, and turned the armies against their leaders. Not till law was obeyed both by soldiers and citizens, till both thought more of duties than of rights, would success be possible. "There are about six millions of men in the country all thinking themselves sovereign and qualified to govern; some thirty-four governors of States who feel like petty kings; and about ten thousand editors,

[1] Carlyle's *Cromwell*, Letter 18, Speech xi.

who presume to dictate to generals,presidents, and cabinets." While Lincoln thought that the issue of the struggle would show whether popular government was an absurdity or not, Sherman thought that the struggle itself was proving it an absurdity. "The Northern people," he said, "have to unlearn all their experience of the past thirty years, and to be born again, before they will see the truth[1]."

In the end, after much suffering and many mistakes, "the Northern people" learnt the conditions of military efficiency and military success—old lessons which the English had learnt at the same cost in the seventeenth century, and may have to learn again in the twentieth.

It is worth while to compare men as well as events, after the manner of Plutarch. At the close of our war Cromwell was in a position very much like that of Grant: a successful general whose victories marked him out for the headship of the State. But it is not with Grant that I shall compare

[1] *The Sherman Letters*, 1894, pp. 148, 162, 166, 190, 199, 211.

Cromwell. Each nation, in its need, produced one man whose figure dominates the time, who seems to incarnate for posterity the ideals of the party which triumphed in the struggle, Cromwell and Lincoln. Lincoln was a statesman, Cromwell a great general as well. Lincoln was a man of the people, Cromwell belonged to the upper classes. "I was by birth a gentleman," he said, "living neither in any considerable height nor yet in obscurity." He believed in class distinctions, "in the ranks and order of men" as he put it, and held the maintenance of these distinctions "a good interest of the nation and a great one," and opposed anything that tended "to the reducing all to an equivalent." Lincoln, on the other hand, said in one of his speeches that he should never be a gentleman "in the outside polish," but as to "that which constitutes the inside of a gentleman" he hoped he was one. He termed himself one of the common people. Once, as he told his secretary, he dreamt that he was in a great assembly which made way to let their President pass. As he passed, someone said, "He is a common looking fellow." In his dream Lincoln turned to the critic and answered, "Friend, the Lord prefers common looking people; that is why he made so many of them." Lincoln always felt that he was one of the many and sympathised with the many, not with the few. His definition of a free government was one "where every man has a right to be equal with every other man."

Cromwell had all the advantages in the way of education that the time could supply—a grammar school, a university, the Inns of Court (though his biographers tell us that he did not carry much away from his university except a little Latin and a taste for athletic exercises). Lincoln was self-educated, and reared in hardships. When a journalist asked him for facts about his early life, he said, "It can all be condensed in a single sentence, and that sentence you will find in Gray's *Elegy*—'The short and simple annals of the poor[1].'" But when one compares the

---

[1] Rhodes, ii. 308, 312; Nicolay and Hay, ix. 355; x. 347.

speeches of the two, it is the self-taught man who seems the educated man. Lincoln's lucid and orderly arrangement of his subject, his clear and cogent logic, his simple yet perfect expression of the thought he wishes to convey, his restraint as well as his eloquence—all these qualities reveal not merely natural gifts, but patient labour, minute study of the best models, acute discrimination of their merits, and severe self-criticism. Cromwell, as he himself frankly owned, was no orator; he was convincing because he made it his business "to speak things," not to "play the orator." An admirer said that he spoke home just as he charged home. One must make allowance for the difference between the instruments Cromwell and Lincoln had to handle: it was more difficult for the best speaker to express things clearly in the involved syntax of the seventeenth century than it was when two centuries of use had simplified the structure of the English sentence. But though Cromwell was capable of hammering out a powerful phrase, and rose sometimes to eloquence, he had little power of orderly and lucid statement. Once when he succeeded in attaining it he said, with a mixture of thankfulness and surprise, "Truly I think it hath pleased God to lead me to a true and clear stating our agreement and our difference[1]."

The difference between the standpoints of Lincoln and Cromwell as rulers comes out very clearly in the expressions they employ. Each regarded himself as the champion of the people. Each used precisely the same phrase about the nation he ruled: both style it "the best people in the world." "Incomparably the best people in the world," said Cromwell, forestalling future comparisons. Cromwell's assertion that his government ruled "for the good of the people, and for their interest, and without respect to any other interest," may be set side by side with Lincoln's statement that his aim was to preserve "the government of the people, for the people, by the people." It is in the last

---

[1] *Clarke Papers*, i. 134, 380.

three words that the difference lies. One can hardly say that Cromwell's aim included government by the people. "What's for their good, not what pleases them" was his motto. Lincoln held that in the long run the people was infallible, but there is no trace of that optimistic view in Cromwell's speeches.

Further, the two men used the word "people" in rather different senses: Lincoln used it with a larger and more inclusive meaning; Cromwell saw in the midst of the English people a smaller body, "a peculiar people," "the people of God," "a people that are to God as the apple of His eye." It was the cause of "the people of God" that he had always in his mind, not that of the people in general, though he held that the interests of the two were not incompatible. Lincoln, when he qualified the word "people," spoke of "the plain people" as his special care, and of himself as their representative. One man thought of a class which included all but the whole nation; the other of a minority consisting of a number of allied sects.

Yet Lincoln was as profoundly religious a man as Cromwell was, though more reticent in the expression of his religious feelings. That was very much the result of the difference between the two ages in which they lived—what was natural and seemly to the Puritans of the seventeenth century would have appeared artificial and indecent to the men of the nineteenth. But there was a difference in the temperament of the two men, and in any age Cromwell would have been more outspoken than Lincoln about such matters. Both men had in early life passed through a period of melancholy caused by religious doubts. In Lincoln there was an underlying strain of sadness which was permanent. But in Cromwell's sanguine nature doubts once settled were settled for ever, and his faith translated itself into sober certainty or an exultant confidence.

Each alike professed his resolve to do in mundane affairs that which appeared to him

the will of God, and both equally distrusted
people who professed to tell them what it
was. A deputation from the various sects
of Chicago once urged Lincoln to issue a
proclamation of universal emancipation at
once. He answered, "I am approached with
the most opposite opinions and advice by
religious men, who are equally certain that
they represent the divine will. I am sure
that either the one or the other class is
mistaken in that belief, and perhaps in some
respects both. I hope it will not be irreverent
for me to say that if it is probable that God
would reveal His will to others, on a point
so directly connected with my duty, it might
be supposed He would reveal it directly to
me; for unless I am more deceived in myself
than I often am, it is my earnest desire to
know the will of Providence in this matter.
And if I can learn what it is, I will do it.
These are not, however, the days of miracles,
and I suppose it will be granted I am not
to expect a direct revelation. I must study
the plain physical facts of the case, ascertain

what is possible, and learn what appears to be wise and right[1]."

Cromwell's attitude was very like Lincoln's. He heard patiently and civilly persons who took upon themselves to tell him what God's will was. But he knew that these beliefs were deceptive things. "We are all of us," he said once, "very apt to call that faith that perhaps may be but carnal imaginations and carnal reasonings." And another time he said: "There may be a carnal confidence, upon misunderstood and misapplied precepts, which may be called spiritual drunkenness." One day in the council of the army an officer declared that the unanimity with which the majority advocated a certain course was the result of a voice from God, and that they ought to hearken unto it. Cromwell replied that he was not unwilling to hear God speaking in any man, but that He was quite as likely to be heard speaking in the report of the committee which they were met to discuss.

[1] Nicolay and Hay, vi. 155.

3—2

God's purpose, according to Cromwell, must be discovered in a different way—in that which He permitted to happen or caused to happen. "Seek to know the mind of God in all that chain of providences," he wrote to Colonel Hammond. Cromwell meant by "dispensations" or "providences" what other people call facts or events. He rebuked the Scots for refusing to recognise the significance of one of these dispensations and "slightingly calling it an event"—it was the event known as the battle of Dunbar[1]. In short, Cromwell's "look at providences" means just the same thing as Lincoln's "look into the plain physical facts of the case." Lincoln too was inclined to regard victories as something more than the result of stronger battalions and more skilful movements. A little after the battle of Antietam he was discussing with his cabinet the expediency of announcing his policy of emancipating the slaves. "In the course of his discussion,"

[1] Carlyle's *Cromwell*, Letters 85, 136, 148; *Clarke Papers*, i. 238, 375.

says a member of his cabinet, "he remarked that he had made a vow—a covenant—that if God gave us the victory in the approaching battle, he would consider it an indication of divine will, and that it was his duty to move forward in the cause of emancipation." So, having gained something like a victory, he kept his vow and issued the proclamation.

Both men, therefore, in spite of formal differences of expression, agreed in their attitude, each striving to see what the fact was and to interpret its meaning, not seeking to impose his own plan as if it were inspired, but accepting with a wise opportunism the guidance of events. "I claim not to have controlled events, but confess that events have controlled me," said Lincoln[1], just as Cromwell confessed that he had risen without knowing where he was going, and "seen nothing in these dispensations long beforehand."

Where Lincoln was superior to Cromwell was in the possession of a calmer and more balanced judgment. He subjected his own

---

[1] Nicolay and Hay, vi. 160; Rhodes, iii. 343, 423.

motives and conduct to a scrutiny that made self-deception hardly possible. He was neither so certain that God was on the side of the North as Cromwell was that God was on the side of the Parliament[1] nor so sure that he could interpret the meaning of events. One of the "plain physical facts of the case" was the opinion of the people; he could interpret that, he was careful to keep in touch with it, and not to advance too fast for it.

Lincoln died at the moment when his cause had triumphed. The captain fell, as a poet said, when the voyage was over and the ship was anchored safe and sound. It was as if Cromwell had fallen when the crowning mercy of Worcester closed the book of war.

If he had died then, Cromwell's fame, though not as spotless as Washington's or Lincoln's, would have been purer than it is. The next seven years gave occasion to half his party to denounce him as an apostate, and to the next generation to regard him as

---

[1] Cf. Nicolay and Hay, vi. 154, 343; Carlyle's *Cromwell*, ed. Lomas, Letter 148.

a tyrant. Mr Roosevelt describes him as a man "cursed with love of power," a man who "had acquired a dictatorial habit of mind." He asserts that "if Cromwell had been a Washington the Puritan revolution might have been made permanent[1]." But to judge thus is to misunderstand the man and the time. There were only two alternatives to Cromwell's rule, anarchy and the restoration of the Stuarts. In America as in England the war was followed by a "reconstruction period," and the task of rebuilding was more difficult than the task of winning battles.

In England it was even more difficult than it was in America. During the American Civil War the constitution was not destroyed as ours was. The Americans had the advantage of retaining the old fabric intact, strengthened rather than weakened by the storm through which it had passed, and needing only a few amendments to adapt it to the new state of things. The instrument

[1] Roosevelt, *Life of Cromwell*, 188, 206.

necessary to carry out the work of reconstruction was ready to their hands.

In England on the contrary the constitution had practically perished in the struggle. All that survived was a part of it, and that a fragmentary part. The cases would have been parallel if the Americans had emerged from the contest without a President or a Senate, and with about a quarter of the Legislature installed as a provisional government and exercising absolute power. But the position of England between 1651 and 1660 was not like that of the Americans in 1865. It was more like that of the Americans between 1783 and 1788. The English had shaken off the yoke of their old government, but had not succeeded in creating a new one, and were in danger of drifting into anarchy just as the Americans were before the adoption of the constitution[1]. Cromwell and the Puritans had the task of making a new constitution and could not succeed in achieving it.

[1] Fiske, *The Critical Period of American History.*

There is another reason why the Americans were more successful in solving the problems that were left them. They had a long experience of the working of democratic institutions, and we were just beginning to make the experiment of republican government. The English of the middle of the seventeenth century, as Mr Roosevelt observes, "had by no means attained to that power of compromise which they showed forty years later in the Revolution of 1688, or which was displayed by their blood-kin and political heirs, the American victors in the struggles of 1776 and 1861[1]."

I will go further and say that the very idea of compromise was as unfamiliar to the average seventeenth-century Englishman as it was familiar to the average citizen of the United States. The constitution of the United States was itself a compromise; not a compromise slowly effected by the incessant and insensible action of opposing forces, as our constitution is, but a compromise made

[1] Roosevelt, *Oliver Cromwell*, p. 100.

purposely and at once by the ingenious statecraft of able legislators. Therefore the political education of the American people in 1865 was far in advance of that of the English people of 1651, and statesmen who sought to heal and reconcile could find in public opinion there a support which was lacking here.

These considerations help to explain how it was that the victorious North used its victory with such moderation. Unexampled the leniency of the American government certainly was. "Never before," declares an American historian, "on the signal failure of so great an attempt at revolution, had a complete victory been attended with no proscriptions, no confiscation of land, no putting of men to death[1]." It was contrasted with the conduct of the Russian government toward the Poles after the attempted revolution of 1830, or of the Austrians towards the Hungarians after that of 1848. It was contrasted with the conduct of the

[1] Rhodes, vi. 49; vii. 174.

English Parliamentarians to the Royalists. In America, Davis and Lee and other leaders escaped scot free, in England the King, four noblemen and a score of gentlemen suffered on the scaffold. This wise clemency of the Americans was partly due to the influence and example of Lincoln. There had been wild talk about inflicting exemplary punishment on the leaders of the rebellion, but one of the last things Lincoln did was to announce his resolution that this should not be. "No one," he said, "need expect he would take any part in hanging or killing these men, even the worst of them. Frighten them out of the country, open the gates, let down the bars, scare them out." When he was urged to take measures to intercept the flight of President Davis he is said to have replied, "I do not see that we have any use for a white elephant." On the other hand we find Cromwell in 1648 urging Parliament to "take courage to do the work of the Lord," so that "they that are implacable and will not leave troubling the land may

43

speedily be cut off out of the land." We
find him telling Fairfax that all his officers
express "a very great zeal to have impartial
justice done upon offenders," and that he
himself is persuaded that this is a thing
"which God puts into our hearts[1]."

It was not that Cromwell and his officers
were by nature more bloodthirsty than Grant
and his officers. The difference in their
tempers was due to the difference in their
ideas. The English people of the seventeenth
century were behind the Americans not only
in their political but in their religious education. Perhaps there was too much of the old
Adam in the Cromwellian officers, certainly
there was too much of the Old Testament.
They were full of horrid texts about punishment and expiation. One of their favourites
was Numbers xxxv. 33. Ludlow quotes it
as his reason for approving the death of the
king. "I was convinced by the express
words of God's law that 'blood defileth a

[1] Nicolay and Hay, x. 203; Putnam, *Abraham Lincoln*,
p. 187; Carlyle's *Cromwell*, Letters 64, 83.

land, and the land cannot be cleansed of the blood that is shed therein, but by the blood of him that shed it.'"

Lincoln too found a text for an answer when he was asked about the punishment of the rebels: it was David's answer, "What have I to do with you, ye sons of Zeruiah? Shall there be any man put to death this day in Israel?" (2 Samuel xix. 22)[1].

Any comparison must also take into account the difference in the duration of the two contests. In America the Civil War lasted from 1861 to 1865 and was never renewed. In England there were two Civil Wars, one lasting from 1642 to 1646, the other from 1648 to 1651. In America the defeated party accepted the result of the war as final: in England they took up arms again and called in the Scots to aid them. After our first Civil War no man suffered on the scaffold for his part in it: the officers of the army were eager for a reconciliation and were disposed to grant the defeated

---

[1] Nicolay and Hay, x. 284; Ludlow, *Memoirs*, i. 207.

royalists better terms than the politicians and civilians of their party thought wise. But after the second Civil War the temper of the officers was changed: they became eager for the punishment of the royalist leaders. Cromwell wrote to Parliament that the fault of those who had taken part in this second war "was certainly double to those who were in the first, because it is the repetition of the same offence against all the witness God hath borne." They had committed a new crime against their country by calling in foreign helpers. "A more prodigious treason than any that had been perpetrated before, because the former quarrel on their part was that Englishmen might rule over one another, this to vassalise us to a foreign nation[1]."

Now supposing that the Confederate leaders had imitated the English royalists, taken up their arms again in 1867, and called in an army of Canadians or Mexicans to help them to overthrow the government

---

[1] Carlyle's *Cromwell*, Letters 62, 82, 84.

of the Republic, is it not likely that Grant's officers would have become as implacable as Cromwell's? Would a second triumph over rebellion have been as stainless as the first?

The good sense and the patriotism of the Southerners deserve the praise of historians no less than the moderation of the North. But as to the treatment of the defeated party by the victors—bating the question of the shedding of blood—were the Southerners so much better treated than the English royalists after all? It is true that there was no confiscation of land as there was after our Civil War. In England a small number of the leading royalists lost the whole of their estates, the rest had to pay fines ranging from one-tenth to one-third of the value of their property. In Ireland, where the struggle was not so much a civil war as a war of races and creeds, the Catholic landowners lost two-thirds of their estates, and had to remove to Connaught to obtain an equivalent for the other third. In America the Southern landowners did not lose their estates, but by the emancipation of their negroes they lost the capital which made their estates productive. Further, during the period of negro misrule which followed the war, land was so overtaxed by the State governments that all through the South farms were sold in thousands for non-payment of taxes. It is said that about one-fifth of the area of Mississippi was in this way forfeited to the State. Financially the results of defeat were more ruinous to the land-owning class in the Southern States than they were to the corresponding class amongst the English royalists.

Politically the position of the ex-Confederate soldiers during the period of reconstruction was far more galling than that of English royalists during the Commonwealth and Protectorate. In England all who had borne arms for the King were disfranchised and disabled from sitting in Parliament or holding municipal office. But the loss of political rights was not aggravated by subjection to the rule of an inferior race. In

America the disfranchisement was only partial. Its effects have been thus defined: "The highest social class, the men of brains, character, and experience were disfranchised"..."Of the whites the illiterate were admitted, the intelligent excluded." At the same time the franchise was given to about 700,000 negroes, though in five States the negro voters outnumbered the whites. "No such mass," says the historian I have just quoted, "of political inexperience, of childish ignorance—no such 'terrible mass of inert domesticated barbarism' was ever before in our country called upon to exercise the suffrage[1]."

As in England no settlement was attained till the old constitution was restored and the disfranchised royalists regained their rights, so in America none was possible till the excluded class were re-enfranchised and the reality of self-government restored to the Southern States.

Each of these settlements left later

---

[1] Rhodes, vi. 82.

generations a problem which it would tax their statesmanship to solve. In both countries wise men blundered when they had to deal with racial questions. We Englishmen have still to reckon with the consequences of the policy of Cromwell and the Puritans in Ireland. Their land confiscations laid, in the words of Mr Lecky, the foundation of that deep and lasting division between the proprietary and the tenants which is the chief cause of the political and social difficulties of Ireland. The people of the United States have still to reckon with the consequences of giving the suffrage to the negro race. We see the temporary evils which resulted from that experiment; we do not know what social or political difficulties it may cause in the future. Neither the gloomy nor the sanguine predictions of contemporary publicists are satisfactory guides; an historian needs the fuller evidence which time alone can bring in order to complete the parallel between the results of the two Civil Wars.